I0756301

FINISHING LINE PRESS
www.finishinglinepress.com

Drinking with the Enemy

poems by

Wayne Karlin

Finishing Line Press
Georgetown, Kentucky

Drinking with the Enemy

For Lucille Clifton and Michael Glaser,
companions of the breakfast table.
Words call us and we go.

ISBN 979-8-89990-462-2 First Edition

ACKNOWLEDGMENTS

"A Day Nothing Happened" in *The Washington Spectator*
"After the War Odysseus Meets Helen" and "Looking at Munch's The Scream on Memorial Day" in *The Raven's Perch*
"As if from Leaves" in *Connections*
"Because You Are Not Here," "Butch in Autumn" and "The Lotus Eaters" in *Vox Populi*
"Coming Home" in *Collateral*
"Drinking with the Enemy," in *Passager*
"Odysseus Descends into the Land of the Dead," in *The Blue Mountain Review*
"Passing Lane" in *WWPH Writes*
"Pornography-1968," in *The Los Angeles Review*
"Singer of Everyday Miracles,: in *Friends Journal*
"The Drinking of the Nước Mắm, Dorchester, Massachusetts," in *Clockhouse*
"The Light Between the Words" in *River Heron Review*
"What Binds Us," in *The Wrath Bearing Tree*

Publisher: Leah Huete de Maines
Editor: Christen Kincaid
Cover painting: At Midnight #14__Nửa đêm by Hà Mạnh Thắng, courtesy of the artist.
Author Photo: Doug Anderson
Cover Design: Wayne Karlin

Order online: www.finishinglinepress.com
also available on amazon.com

Author inquiries and mail orders:
Finishing Line Press
PO Box 1626
Georgetown, Kentucky 40324
USA

Contents

PART ONE:
DRINKING WITH THE ENEMY

Drinking with the Enemy

"Abstract words such as glory, honor, courage, or hallow were obscene beside the concrete names of villages, the numbers of roads, the names of rivers, the numbers of regiments and the dates."

—Ernest Hemingway, *A Farewell to Arms*

I was the only American at the table. We were all veterans.
Christmas evening in Hong Gai. In the war, one of the men said,
you bombed the church here. He laughed uproariously.
It still doesn't have a roof, he said. A red plastic Santa Claus

and a green plastic Christmas tree stood in the lobby. We played a
drinking game with glasses of beer. At the count of three everyone
had to drain his glass. If he couldn't he had to drink another glass.
We drank to empty ourselves, a film run in reverse. The man sitting

to my right smiled at me, gently, tentatively. Like many who had
been in in the war his teeth were bad, brown-stained and broken.
His skin was pitted and lined with the years we shared and didn't
share and he walked slightly hunched over, like a farmer looking
down at his earth,

or like a man in a rice field crouching under the sound of my
helicopter rotors. ở đâu? he asked me. Then: Where? It was his
only English word. He tapped his chest with the carapaced fingers
of his farmer's hand, trying to dislodge the two questions we all
asked each other and the two questions we didn't.

When? Where? Did you try to kill me there? Did I try to kill you then?
I took his hand and pushed it against my chest. Quảng Nam,
Thừa Thiên Huế, Quảng Trị, I said. He grabbed my other hand and
pushed it against his chest. I could feel his heart beating hard through
the skin of my palm.

Quảng Trị, Quảng Trị, Quảng Trị, he said. One of the other veterans
yelled một, hai, ba, yo! We drained our glasses ten times. Nine of them
for nine years the man to my right was there longer than I. His eyes grew
desperate. His farmer's hand was trembling. He pointed at his filled

glass, pointed to his mouth, tapped his forehead hard with his blunt,
callused finger. Quảng Trị, Quảng Trị, Quảng Trị, he said, tapping

violently to dislodge the seepage flowing with the beer into his brain, pushing heavily into the cavities of his heart. I took the glass of the man to my right from him and I drank it for him, into myself, all of it, for him. It nested in my chest, an icy stone.

Uống cùng kẻ thù   Drinking with the Enemy

Translated by Ngô Xuân Hiền

"Những từ ngữ trừu tượng như vinh quang, danh dự, lòng can đảm, hay sự linh thiêng trở nên thật phản cảm khi đặt cạnh tên cụ thể của những ngôi làng, số hiệu những con đường, tên những dòng sông, số hiệu trung đoàn và những ngày tháng."
—Ernest Hemingway, Giã từ vũ khí

Tôi là người Mỹ duy nhất ngồi tại bàn.
Tất cả chúng tôi đều là cựu binh.
Đêm Giáng sinh ở Hồng Gai. Trong chiến tranh, một người đàn ông nói,
các ông đã ném bom nhà thờ ở đây. Anh ấy cười thành tiếng.
Nhà thờ vẫn chưa có mái, anh nói.
Một ông già Noel bằng nhựa đỏ
và một cây thông Giáng sinh nhựa xanh đứng nơi sảnh khách sạn.
Chúng tôi chơi trò thách uống bằng những cốc bia.
Khi đếm đến ba, mọi người phải uống cạn ly.
Nếu ai không thể, người đó phải uống thêm ly nữa.
Chúng tôi uống để trút rỗng chính mình, như một bộ phim quay ngược.
Người đàn ông ngồi bên phải mỉm cười với tôi, nhẹ nhàng, thăm dò.
Như nhiều người từng kinh qua cuộc chiến, hàm răng anh đã hỏng, ố nâu
và sứt mẻ.
Da anh rỗ và hằn dấu những năm tháng chúng tôi từng chia sẻ, và cả những
năm tháng không.
Anh đi hơi khom lưng, như một người nông dân nhìn xuống mảnh đất của
mình,
hay như một người trên ruộng lúa đang náu mình dưới tiếng động cơ trực
thăng của tôi.
"Ở đâu?" anh hỏi tôi. Rồi: "Where?"
Đó là từ tiếng Anh duy nhất anh biết.
Anh vỗ vào ngực mình bằng những ngón tay chai cứng như mai rùa của
người làm ruộng,
cố gắng bật ra hai câu hỏi tất cả chúng tôi đều dành cho nhau, và hai câu hỏi
chúng tôi không bao giờ thốt ra:
Khi nào? Ở đâu? Anh có cố giết tôi ở đó không? Tôi có cố giết anh lúc đó
không?

Tôi cầm lấy tay anh và áp nó vào ngực mình.
Quảng Nam, Thừa Thiên Huế, Quảng Trị, tôi nói.
Anh chộp lấy bàn tay kia của tôi và áp nó vào ngực anh.
Tôi có thể cảm thấy trái tim anh đập mạnh qua lớp da nơi lòng bàn tay
mình.
Quảng Trị, Quảng Trị, Quảng Trị, anh nói.

Một người cựu binh khác hô lớn: Một, hai, ba, dzô!
Chúng tôi uống cạn ly mười lần.
Chín ly trong số đó dành cho chín năm ròng người đàn ông bên phải tôi đã ở lại nơi ấy lâu hơn tôi.
Mắt anh trở nên tuyệt vọng. Bàn tay nông dân của anh run rẩy.
Anh chỉ vào ly bia đầy, chỉ vào miệng mình, gõ mạnh vào trán bằng ngón tay thô ráp, chai sạn.
Quảng Trị, Quảng Trị, Quảng Trị, anh nói,
vỗ mạnh như để đẩy những ký ức đang rỉ ra cùng dòng bia vào não bộ,
ép sâu vào những ngăn tim.
Tôi cầm lấy ly bia từ tay người đàn ông bên phải,
và tôi uống thay anh, uống vào trong mình, uống cạn, vì anh.
Nó kết lại trong ngực tôi, một viên đá lạnh.

As if from Leaves

for Lê Minh Khuê

At fifteen
she'd run away to
join the army
To fight you, she said
She'd never been this close
to an American before.
I was nineteen, I said
Once, she said
she'd spied on G.I.'s
bathing near Khe Sanh
needing to see them
unshelled and human
but they were too far away,
she couldn't see anything.
You were ghosts to us too, I said.
The helicopters scared her
the most, she said
They came down.
I know, I said
and thought of how
differently each of us
heard those three words,
and then thought of
her crouching under
jungle canopy,
the downward arc
the red flashes of my tracers
the strangeness of connection.

Twenty and more years before
I had searched for her
on the ground
as she had searched for me
in the air
our eyes aching with
the need to see.
But I didn't see her
beneath the green canopy
the mists twisting
like ghosts
against dark mountains
and she didn't see me
in the stir of treetops
the light shivering
like panic
through the branches,
until now
as simply
as forgetting
a dream
we looked
and our faces emerged
as if from leaves,
as if from sky.

The Drinking of the Nước Mắm, Dorchester, Massachusetts

The rocking chairs groaned and creaked, bobbing back and forth like Jews in prayer. The name of the prayer was I'm glad I met you now and not then. We could hear gunshots from drive-bys echoing from the grave of the past. The older Vietnamese poet poured gin into our glasses and his own. I didn't kiss a woman until I was thirty years old, he said. The younger Vietnamese poet lit our cigarettes. The woman writer who filled in craters after we bombed the Hồ Chí Minh Trail stroked the air above the table, smoothing earth over the war. We ate cucumbers, dipping them into a saucer filled with nước mắm which is made from the fermenting corpses of fish. The insides of our mouths wept. We tasted red mud and fire and bitter cordite and brass. Gunshots rolled into our ears from Dorchester, from Quảng Nam, from Quảng Trị. The dead stood behind our chairs, pushing down on their backs to make us rock. The fuck you drinking with, they whispered into our ears. The two bottles of gin and the bottle of vodka were empty. The older poet picked up the bottle of nước mắm and filled our glasses and smiled at me from the turret of a tank. Decay stung my nostrils. The tangled dead on the deck of my helicopter filled my mouth. I told my friend it was a ceremony. The dead hooted, pushed on the backs of our chairs, rocking them harder and harder. My friend tasted smashed kids run over by a six-by driver for shits and giggles. The woman writer's eyes raked my face. On the Trail she buried the dead. The bombs blew off clothes and she was ashamed to be found naked so she did not die. The older poet grinned like a skull. The hands of the naked dead clutched our shoulders, shaking us like puppets as we drank the war long into the night.

What Binds Us

I spent twenty-six years
in the jungle;
I was thirty years old
before I kissed a woman,
the Vietnamese poet said
and stared at
the American veterans
as if amazed at
what he had kissed instead.

In the war, he said,
his comrades had covered
his body with their own
to protect him
from the bombs
so he could finish
writing his poem,
although now
in his country
he fears there's no one
who will understand
the language
in which it was written

Looking at Munch's *The Scream* on Memorial Day

I fear some words, if spoken,
would tremble panic through your skin
or worse, a shudder of revulsion,
wake a fear lodged waiting in the ancient
hollowed memory of your bones.
This is an unspoken poem.
This is a three in the morning poem.
This is the unscreamed scream
that echoes in the chamber of my mouth.
This is a silent poem.
This is the silence that seals
the lip of a wound.

A Day Nothing Happened

We would take a 6-by truck into An Tan from Ky Ha, to buy soda or beer or sex. A line of little thatched-roof kiosks, some of them walled with flattened beer cans from our trash dumps, strung along a dirt road rutted with landmine craters, a cloud of reddish dust hanging perpetually over it. I was standing with some other Marines in the scant shade of a scraggly areca tree, buying dusty bottles of soda from the girls who sold them from the baskets they carried. I joked with one girl maybe eight years old; she had a dirty face and a beautiful smile. She wanted to try out her English with me, and I was correcting her pronunciation: No, say moth-er-fuck-er, not motha fucka. An amtrack—the name Marines had for the massive thirty-two ton amphibious tracked vehicles that the army called Armored Personnel Carriers—clanked to a halt nearby, and the girl ran over and lifted her basket high over her head like an offering to the gods of war. A Marine, deeply tanned, his utilities and helmet and skin covered with fine red powder that was reamed on his face with rivulets of sweat, leaned over and snatched a bottle from the girl, knocked its cap off on the edge of the vehicle, drained the foaming coke. 100 p's, the girl yelled up at him. 100 piastres. What she was owed. He stared at her. 100 p's, she screamed. He threw the bottle at her, hard and fast; she stepped to the side as it whizzed past her head, planted her legs apart, stared up at him. Her shirt was ragged, held by one button. Her chest was heaving. 100 p's, she insisted. Leave, I thought. Get out of there, kid. The amtrack was scored with bullet rakings, battered, its tracks caked with mud; the men on it staring out with flat indifference or with that crazy grunt light in their eyes. The Marine took out a .45, leaned over the side again and pointed it at the girl's forehead. I didn't move. A tableau: girl, maybe eight years old or maybe nine or maybe older; amtrack, thirty-two ton; Marine, .45. Di-di, you little gook bitch, he said. Moth-er fuck-er, she said clearly. 100 p's. He racked the handgun. She didn't move. 100 p's, she screamed up at him. Di-di mau, he said, and pushed the handgun closer. My M-14 was slung with the barrel forward and down so it could be brought up quickly and I moved my finger to the trigger. I remember the wet slick feel of the trigger under my skin. I still feel it. I could feel his finger was tightening on his trigger as, or because, my finger was tightening on mine. The girl's hands gripped the basket, her eyes locked to the Marine's. I understood she would die rather than move. I understood that we would lose the war. The realization was as clear as if someone had spoken a sentence into my ears. We will lose the war. For shit sake, a voice with a thick, weary Southern accent said from the amtrack, and a skinny Marine leaned over the side and dropped a hundred piaster note to the ground. It fluttered near the girl's feet. She didn't look at it. The other Marine shook his head in disgust, snorted, pulled up the pistol. The girl remained where she was. After a while, she bent down and took the money. I turned away and went back to my friends. It had been a day when nothing happened

Pornography-1968

Nights he sat in a concrete box of an apartment on Ventura Boulevard, watching his war in silent black and white on a ten-inch television screen, a disembodied eye on a pressed-wood dresser.

Days he took classes at a community college and worked a job the State of California employment office had gotten for him at the warehouse of a pornography publisher in the Valley. He stood alone in a cavernous warehouse in Van Nuys pulling covers decorated with pictures of splayed women off magazines returned from adult book stores, so that the publisher could recycle them. The covers were printed without dates. Shelves pressed all around him, stacked boxes of paperbacks: The Sexual Habits of College Coeds, Secrets of the SS Brothels, Backdoor Delights, Candystripe Confessions, written by housewives and retirees from the Valley who used academic titles and the names of local streets for their pen names. Dr. Sherman Way, PhD. The magazine titles were more direct, turned to the East: Slanty Sluts, Anal Asians, Oriental Orifices. He got it. Mentally edited the titles down to their true meaning. Gook, Dink. The women's eyes on the covers raked him. He lay his hands over them, pushed them down. He was the Manual Stripper, abbreviated as M.S, on the company's orientation sheet. His M.O.S.—Military Occupational Specialty—is M.S, he told himself. He would pick up a carton of magazines from the floor and put it on a long table, take out one magazine, pull the front and rear cover to one side with his left hand, hold down the body of the magazine with the palm of his right and the weight of his body, and neatly pull off the cover. Bing-bang, the past was gone. That easy. He'd put the stripped magazine (SM) into another box. He stood at his table stripping covers. Someone else would re-cover them. It wasn't his job. The women looked up at him, their eyes accusing. He put his palm against their faces, their breasts, their pink and pearly genitals, and pushed. He couldn't separate them from the dead. They piled around his legs, clung to his knees on the deck of his helicopter. Hot casings from his machine gun showered them. They entwined, bleeding into each other, reaching up, clutching at his knees. How had he gotten here? He was an unlinked bullet. Tossed from the belly of a helicopter into the belly of a C-147, into America,

into waking up one dazed morning utterly alone in a ten by twelve studio apartment in a small complex of stacked concrete boxes between two gas stations on Ventura Boulevard in Tarzana: a linty, purplish rug, a monk's bed, a black velvet Keene picture, a chipped desk and bureau, and a black and white TV. Shadows from his war played on it, grainy, nebulous. Robert Kennedy died on it live one midnight, in the same lambent light. How had he gotten here? What the fuck had all that been about? Where was everybody? Streams of traffic passed indifferently outside his window, shadow people on their way to shadow lives, oblivious to the shadows pressing weightlessly against them on their seats, the open mouths pressed against all the windows. The driver and their passengers cursed rubbed frantically, with their sleeves with handkerchiefs with the flats of their hands, at the mist, the women's breath, the breath of the dead spreading over the glass, distorting Ventura Boulevard, the shapes of gas stations, fast food restaurants car dealerships diffused through mist, flickering apart, braiding into other shapes, into eyes formed out of fire and palm fronds and sunlight sharp as knives, into eyes that disappeared when the drivers strained to see them but lingered in the corner of their visions. He had the photos he'd taken in Vietnam developed, bought albums, spent sleepless nights arranging and rearranging photographs, tearing them off and re-pasting them and ripping them away again and pressing them back down as they pressed stigmata up into his palms, again and again and always there, and in the morning the women always waited with their eyes.

PART TWO:
LETTERS TO A V.A. DOCTOR FROM THE WAR ON TERROR

Ouroboros

November 11, 2004

Dear Child of God

What do you want me to tell you? What do you want to hear? What do you want me to write? What do you want to see, smell, taste, feel? The wasteland that stretched to the horizon, hot sand spiraling up into dust devils? The garden of wreckage? OK. All yours. Here you go. All the way, as they say or pray or slay. Get to it. Stride into it like an armored angel. A weapon with a weapon. The heat like another layer of heavy Kevlar. You enter the blessed shade of date trees with the others, and you kneel and then lay flat at the spring, the cold, cold water of the oasis softening your cracked lips. Taste it. When you are finished drinking you stand next to a date tree and stretch out your arms, the wood pressed hard into your back. Can you feel it? Do you see the other men sitting in a semi-circle around you, how one by one they rise and come to you, whisper into your ear, asking a perverse absolution? Forgive me, Father, for I did not burn, they say. Forgive me, Father, for I did not stab. Forgive me, Father, for I hesitated. Forgive me, Father, for I didn't pull the trigger. Forgive me, Father, for I saw myself in my enemy's face. Forgive me, Father, for I showed mercy. Forgive me, Father, for I forgave. Never mind, you say. One by one you forgive them their trespasses, place a sweet date on each tongue. I bless you, get some, you say. I bless you, get some, you laugh. I bless you, get some, you scream. As if your scream has called it, you feel something slide into your boot and wrap around your ankle and then rise and tighten around your thigh, its tongue flicking upwards towards your loins and now, this time, you let yourself relax and accept it as it penetrates through your pores, glides up through your veins, binds around the muscle of your heart, squeezing in rhythm until it is in charge of the beat and then continues up the stem of your spine and breaks through a membrane and into your hindbrain, joining what is already there waiting coiled in the convolutions of the cerebellum, settling behind your eyes, narrowing your pupils, swelling inside your skull as you rise, the carapace of your armor clicking like scales around you.

all yours,

Ouroboros

There It Us

May 30, 2005
Dear Doc-tor Feel-good.
I remember the first time we met. Every fucking word. Got some? I ask you. Get some, got some, son, says you, reaching your hand through the skin of my chest, squeezing my heart.

There it is, says you.

Talking some O.G. Nam talk.

I bring you peace, says you.

Yep. You deliver.

Take it.

You bet.

Tell me again about your friend..

Why? He gone.

But not forgotten.

He gone. Long gone Don. Do de done gone Don, we'd sing, the guys in the Bradley with me. Done de done gone Don, daaa! That's how we rolled. More E.S.G. Elementary School Gangsta. The treads on the Bradley go round and round, round and round. Round and round.

Do you think it appropriate to joke about his death?

The joke was on him. And then the joke was on me. All over me. The yoke of the joke. So Oki-doke.

How was that for memory re-ten-tion? TBI my ass. So, OK, here it is Dr. Feelgood. The price of the feel. My very own After Action Report as you want me to call it. As if. The white building. You never saw white until you saw it in that sun. It wasn't a color. It wasn't even the absence of a color. It was alive. I mean it fucking pulsed. Just before it became the sun. Memory reconstruction, that's what you want, right? You ever try to re-con-struct a friend from memory? Like where this part go? Where this one? Slippery as fuck. Slimy as duck. Slithery as suck. But I protect the men I protect the machine I am Death the Destroyer, I scream; shit, man, Don laughs, you Conan the Barbarian, says Don, Don-de-done-gone-Don and I touch the butterfly trigger with a butterfly touch and press and the vibe of the gun moves from my hands to my arms to my shoulders to my shaky breaky mother-fucky heart.

Is that what you need to get me what I need? There it is, doc. There it Us. For your reading pleasure.
cheers,
me

No Place for a Woman

May 28th 2006
Dear Doctor Vulture
How could I do it? I think I understand you. It's not so much you want me to write to you as you want to be written upon. As I once did. You want to be a tabula rasa inscribed with red letters. I get it. Think of it, you said, as a creative writing prompt. Were you mocking me, mocking my dead dreams? My dead writer dead dreams of being a dead writer. No matter. Write what you know, right? The mantra. Moment by moment. Present tense for immediacy. OK. I walk down a dank, dark corridor. It is no place for a woman say the other soldiers. My colleagues. My buddies. A dare. A test. Iron bars press against my skin even though I am not in the cells. The ammoniac stink of piss and shit stings my nostrils. My eyes water. It is no place for a human being. It is no place for a dog. In the cells chained men cringe when they see me. Their eyes meet mine and flit away and they try to bring their hands down to cover their shame. It is no place for a woman, their eyes say. A new group has already been piled in the center of the floor, one atop the other, all gaping assholes and shriveled dicks like photos of corpses in ditches, but alive. Sobbing in humiliation. It is no place for me. Present tense for immediacy. I am not here. It is no place. It cannot exist. It does not exist. It never existed. Past tense for wishful thinking. It will not exist. Future tense for futility. I push it down and try to push it down. I try to fill myself with shame at their humbling. I feel the pistol heavy at my side and the stares on the back of my neck mybudsmyarmymycountryyaah! and the club in my hands now and the power over these poor forked creatures who, yes! wrap their own women in cloth prisons, cut off without mercy whatever their women bare in sunlight, slice away the arcs of their noses to leave grotesque craters, as if all they want are holes. And I bring my club down again and again on that loathsome flesh.

There. There. It. Is. Vulture. There I am was will be. Is that what you wanted to know? Take it. It is the price you asked me for. Take it, my dear Dr. Carrion. It's all yours, motherfucker.

PART THREE: ODYSSEUS

After the War Odysseus Meets Helen

After war they sat across from each other
over loaves of bread that lay on the table between
them like corpses still warm with a linger of life,
like the baked bricks of a burnt city.

She had been a shadow in his mind,
in all their minds,
all who would invent themselves
in her rescue or punishment,
all who had found what she wanted
was not saving, but freedom, her
face and smile mocking them like
a flag fluttering on a distant rampart.
That smile they saw twisted on the lips
of their dead;
that smile they came to see
on the face of their own death.

Now he looked at her behind the slight veil of smoke
rising from the bread and saw she was too small
to hold all of it and he saw his own image reflected
in her eyes, Odysseus who came in the Belly of the Horse,
burner of cities, Nightmare, Nemesis, a howl heard
through thick walls,
sitting before warm bread in a tent, after war,
as she was sitting,
she who had burnt for love and he who had burnt for love,
sitting with the burnt city between them.
She touched him, traced his features as if drawing them,
needing to shape him out of scream and shadow, out of
nightmare and into flesh and form.
And she smiled and her face broke from its legend.
And he broke like a cracked pillar.
He who had become a stone
barely warm with the linger of fire.

Coming Home

Lashed to his mast, his back to wood again as in the Horse,
the dead of Troy screaming and swirling like furies around his head,
he tried to dream an island where he had never been.

His mind broke like a ship from the pull of the Sirens and
he leaned against the rope and felt the splinters
from the mast unsheathing from his shoulders,
easing out like cries of the dead.

Odysseus Descends into the Land of the Dead

Even here the wall. Everything before it mist. Everything after it mist.

Everyone before it mist. Everyone after it mist. The crenelated ridge bristling with spears and mocking faces. Spun into myth by lying bards. Into mist. The bisection

of his life. He shakes the vision from his head. This is not the wall of Troy. It is the wall of Hades. The wall of the dead. It is black and smooth and mirrored and stretches to the horizon. It does not narrow to a point of perception. It

continues, circling the world. Ouroboros. It is a black band that presses against his eyes. It is a black mirror that swallows him as he draws closer. His reflection merciless. Aged. Creped neck, sagging balls. Scribbled over by the names carved in white letters into the

black mirror of the wall. The names of the dead write themselves on his skin, across his forehead, his chest. The white names carve themselves into his skin. Their barbed letters rake his face like the nails of women. Tangle together like discarded clothing on the deck

of his ship. Trench fire into his skin. Odysseus the Cunning, Destroyer of Cities. Offerings line the base of the wall. A dove with its throat cut. A pack of cigarettes. A bottle of beer. A gutted daughter. A pack of condoms. A pair of dog tags. The offerings

fade, return as the dead themselves, draining into the dirt, their faces covered with rubber ponchos against sudden rain. It washes his skin, churns the earth at the base of the wall into red mud. The dead are all wearing his boots. His body strains against its need to step

back, step away. He pushes against it, forward, as he would in battle. The corpses cave into themselves, into the earth, into dust that puffs up and settles in the creases on his face. He steps through the wall into the land of the dead.

He will learn to fit himself, silent as moss, to the embrace of stone.

He will learn to become moss, which is stone dreaming of life.

The Lotus Eaters

And so he returned to Ithaca:
walked naked from the sea
and saw his shadow
fall on the white marble
of the palace:
A soldier's shadow
diminishing as he drew
closer
hunching as if years
piled onto his shoulders
with each step,
and malicious suitors
shaped the seaweed
dripping from him into
a crown of madman's
hair for the parade of
the King of Fools.
He stopped then and
looked at the
glass rock Calypso
had given him,
clutched in his hand
still, after his
long swim
and he saw in its depths
a milky mist parting
to the years ahead.
Tell again about Troy,
Odysseus, Penelope says,
still knitting his shroud
and Telemachus makes a face
and tries on a new robe
as the courtiers nudge each other
and cover their yawns
with soft palms,
their manicured fingers
fluttering
and he can see in their eyes
they don't believe
men could sit in the dark
waiting to be devoured by
a monster who would tear
their limbs and rip their faces
with his rotten teeth,
splinter their bones with the force
of his bite into razoring shards
that would fly through the dark
like beaked furies to slice
the life out of others.
Or that random death
could snap out of the air
and snatch some men from their
seats and leave others
alive next to them
out of no virtue but chance.
Or that men could turn into pigs.
Or that red slaughter would bloom
from wounded love.
Or that men yearning for
home and hearth and the
touch of woman and child
could tear down walls
and burn homes and
rend the mirrored flesh
they held in their own hearts
as if punishing themselves
for having hearts.
Or that men would burn a city and its children
out of a dream of freedom and love.
Or that a man could come home
dripping out of the sea
and bearing the funeral
pyre of thousands
burning on his back and
neck and thousands of burnt
offerings still twisting behind
his eyes, writhing in his
brain like smoke.
And Odysseus knew then
he had come to the Land
of the Lotus Eaters.

PART FOUR:
ELEGIES

Passing Lane

For Rachel

As you drove me home from the hospital,
we didn't speak of my heart.
I was heart sick. Sick of my heart.

Probed, monitored, prodded
to beat in acceptable rhythms, to harden,
to shed grief like a dog shaking off water.

We spoke of your heart.
Of past love, bad love, divorce,
bad endings, the loss of love,

the loss of hope, the need of hope,
the futility of hope, the uncertainty of hope.
The need to leave. To find a way for your heart

to beat in rhythm with your life.
The fear of leaving. The fear of age.
Of loneliness. Of time.

Time gone, time looming before your eyes,
uncertain as tomorrow.
Until our conversation was cut

by the blind swerve of a pickup truck
so stacked with furniture it seemed to be fleeing
panicked from a life pressed in too tight.

Your life, manifested but not metaphoric,
looming larger than time in my window.
You saved us.   You saved yourself.

As you always will. Calmly. Steering
into the precise space you needed.
Your capable hands on the wheel.

Butch in Autumn

For Butch

When she was a pup in autumn
I watched her dive in mad exuberance
into the leaf-filled roadside ditch
and submarine down its length
spraying a delirious scarlet wake
and stop at its far end,
at the edge of wonder,
and look back at me
as if exasperated at my bipedal slowness,
as if to say, where are you?

Those legs gave out yesterday
nearly the last item on whatever final checklist
her body is going through now
and she stares at me,
chin on my knees,
her eyes suddenly older than mine,
heavy with a certain wisdom.
Run ahead again,
old friend,
I'll catch up with you later.

Face Time with my Grandchildren, October 7th, 2023

For the grandchildren of Israel and Gaza

I have to fix my smile onto my face,
to not let
their faces tremble into
the faces of the grandchildren
of Beeri, of Kfar Aza, of Nir Oz,
of Magen, which means shield,
the faces of the grandchildren
of the kibbutzim strung along
the merciless border between worlds,
to not hear
in their singing laughter
the jubilant roar
of the grandchildren
in a desert festival, wild as the crowd at the foot of Sinai,
humming loudly with their fingers pressed into their ears
to block the harsh noise rising all around them louder
and louder until hope and peace collapse
like a failed smile,
to not see
the faces of those children,
their songs keening into the ancient wail,
in the faces of my grandchildren,
to struggle
to see the faces of
my grandchildren in the faces
of the grandchildren
of Khan Yunis, of Jabalya,
of Rafah, which means compassion,
their grandchildren,
those other grandchildren
held and pressed
against the fence of hopelessness,
to see them
beyond the Pale
where our grandparents also stood helpless at the edge
of an endless black ditch, the cold metal on their necks.
their eyes closed,
their lips pressed tight.

Singer of Everyday Miracles

For Michael Glaser

"More war poems?" you said to me, before you were gone.
"More kids and grandkids and food and love-making and love and honey and almonds and everyday miracles? The political can be personal too," I said to you, before you were gone.

"Every time I met with Michael he either taught me something or told me something I needed to know," Matt said to me, after you were gone.

You called me two nights before
a little later than usual.
A little later than we knew it was
A little later than we thought it could be.
Your voice was urgent
with questions
what we needed to know
what we needed to say
what we needed to do
in these days of reluctant mercy
and malevolent faith.
You had no answers
nothing to teach or tell.
You had not called for answers
only for connection
an echo to shatter
isolate silence
before sleep
before that long sleep
before that tender embrace into the
arms of grace
you called to and merged with
as gently as you foretold
as gently as you wished,
leaving me void
of what you could teach me
of what I needed to know
you poet
you singer of
everyday miracles.

I'm losing words everywhere

For Ohnmar Thein Karlin
9/29/1950 - 2/28/2020

I'm losing words everywhere.
The other day I misplaced serendipitous
which would have been ironic if I hadn't lost that word also.
Tuesday scatological was gone, which was shitty,
and on Wednesday I lost juddering and bevel.
Thursday elongate was gone but
I found them all again Saturday,
in a corner of my son's bedroom, near
some discarded Masters of the Universe figures,
He-Man and She-Ra in a dusty box under his bed,

the lost words suddenly forming into themselves in my brain
as if they had never left, right at the instant
I pushed the little button that made Ram Man's neck
elongate obscenely, something that, serendipitously,
I suppose, and not ironically, brought back my wife and I
laughing at that juddering plastic arousal,
as she elbowed me not to, not in front of the kid.

In the end maybe I will forget her name. Her face is already fading
or sometimes streaming into a succession of its changes
over fifty years, each face blossoming from the other
like forgotten words suddenly rediscovered
in another room of my life,

or in a room I have yet to enter, a waiting room
where no words wait, only a silent anticipation
felt on my skin like the breath of her touch.

Because You Are Not Here

For Ohnmar

Clothes that touched your skin
cling for a desperate second
on the metal maw of the donation bin,
tumble into darkness

But when I come home
you return with me, awakened
in a saffron spill of light
on the kitchen counter

The wood molding splintered
by the turn of a wheel-chair
at the bathroom door.

The medicine cabinet opening to
an audience of empty pill bottles
their faint rattle a mockery of applause.

The tight hollow of silence
in the bedroom, in the chest,
in the narrow of the throat.

Because you are not here
you are always here

Because you will never be here
you are always here.

The Light between the Words

For Ohnmar

Afterwards he moved through the world not as in a dream
but as a man imitating the movement of a man in a dream.
He constructed a room from memory near a park in Belgrade,
in Beo-grad, in the white city, white light dancing through
yellowed gauze curtains as if through autumn leaves light flickering
like the light of memory like the light in Jerusalem that blushed
blood under the skin of ancient stone like the skin of lovers
bruised by the heavy press of history, pressed by the kiss of time.
He put himself back in the room and he put her back and lived
in a loop run over and over, rewound, paused, he was afraid
if he stopped it would burn, a spot of flame would flare
in the center of the frame from the very place their bodies
were joined and widen swiftly in a fiery circle and he felt that
circle widen in his stomach and chest like the burn of grief the
burn of absence. He was a man of words but in that room they
spoke in look and breath and touch and didn't know which was
echo and which was source. They spoke in the language of a country
that no longer existed and of a city in that country and of a street
in that city and of a building in that street and of a room in that
building and the words for the world were gone and now he had
to learn to search for her in the light between the words.

Wayne Karlin is an author, editor, and teacher. His books include three works of non-fiction: *Wandering Souls: Journeys With the Dead and the Living in Viet Nam* (Nation Books, 2009) which was also published in translation in Vietnam as *Những linh hồn phiêu dạt* ((Nha Xuat Ban Thong Tan, 2013); *War Movies* (Curbstone, 2005), *Rumors and Stones* (Curbstone, 1996), a collection of short fiction, *Memorial Days: Viet Nam Stories, 1973-2022,* (Texas Tech University Press, 2023); nine novels: The Genizah Publerati, 2024), *A Wolf by the Ears* (University of Massachusetts Press, 2020), *Marble Mountain* (Curbstone, 2007), *The Wished-for Country* (Curbstone, 2002), *Prisoners* (Curbstone, 1998), *US* (Henry Holt, 1993), *The Extras* (Henry Holt, 1989); *Lost Armies* (Henry Holt, 1988), and *Crossover* (Harcourt Brace, 1984), (also published in England (Methuen, 1985), and in translation in Sweden, Finland, Italy and Holland), and a poetry chapbook: *Drinking with the Enemy*, 2026. After service in the United States Marine Corps in the Vietnam War, Karlin co-edited the first collection of Vietnam veterans' fiction from the war, *Free Fire Zone: Short Stories by Vietnam Veterans,* in 1973, and in 1995 was the co-editor, with Lê Minh Khuê and Truong Vu of the first collection of fiction by Vietnamese and American authors who had been on different sides in the war: *The Other Side of Heaven: Postwar Fiction by Vietnamese and American Writers.* He became the pro bono American editor of the Curbstone Press Voices from Vietnam series and introduced, adapted and edited novels and short story collections by contemporary Vietnamese authors, as well as a second anthology. Karlin was ALSO one of the script writers, a technical consultant, and acted in the feature film *Song of the Stork,* a Vietnamese-Singaporean co-production (Megamedia, PTE, BHD Productions, 2002) which has won the Best Feature Film Award at the Milano Film Festival in 2002 and has been shown in other festivals in Belgium, Canada, the U.S. and Thailand. In 2006 and 2009 Karlin was a consulting producer and writer for *Shared Weight,* a series of hour-long radio programs involving interviews with American and Vietnamese writers, film makers and artists in the U.S. and in Vietnam, and journeys of reconciliation, produced by the Center for Emerging Media for National Public Radio. It was broadcast on over 40 NPR stations and is still in circulation. Karlin retired as Professor Emeritus from the College of Southern Maryland in 2017, after thirty-one years of service.

www.ingramcontent.com/pod-product-compliance
Lightning Source LLC
LaVergne TN
LVHW090539110826
845146LV00003B/1172

* 9 7 9 8 8 9 9 9 0 4 6 2 2 *